D1563783

To: Barb

From:
Elissa

MODERNes

Songs of the Heart © 1997 Theresa and Erika Carter. All rights reserved. Printed in Singapore. No part of this book may be used or reproduced in any manner whatsoever without written permission except in the case of reprints in the context of reviews. For information write Andrews McMeel Publishing, an Andrews McMeel Universal company, 4520 Main Street, Kansas City, Missouri 64111.

ISBN: 0-8362-5102-4

Songs of the Heart

Art by Theresa and Erika Carter
Written by Michael Anderson

**Andrews McMeel
Publishing**

Kansas City

A song of the
heart, for
you my
kindred spirit...

The years

have held

so much

for us...

...our memories

are full

and rich.

We

celebrate

simple

pleasures...

sharing

hopes

and

dreams.

And

when doubts

and

fears

threatened...

our friendship

was a harbor

against

the storm.

Ours has been

an ageless bond,

forged of

grand moments

and precious miracles...

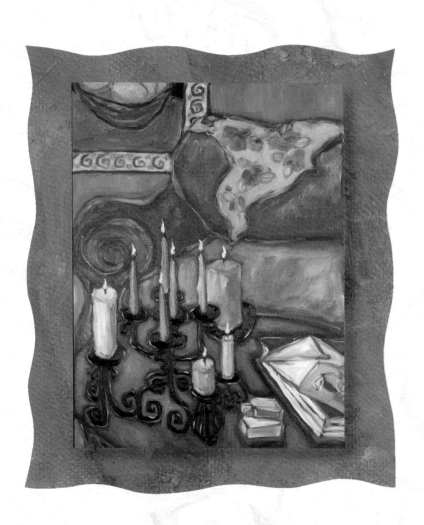

...linking

us to

the rhythm

of life.

Time after time,

our worn

footsteps

bring us home...

to a comfortable

place where

friendship fills us

with music and light...

...a symphony
of
renewal...

and our

souls soar

beyond

the stars

and moon.

We are,
we will always be,
kindred spirits...
listening to
the songs
of the heart.

t. Carter

The Carter sisters: Theresa and Erika

The Modernes greeting books feature
the modern impressionistic artwork of
sisters and fellow artists, Theresa and
Erika Carter. The Carter sisters are
second generation Santa Barbarans
from a large and artistic family.
As children they were surrounded by a
wide variety of art, cultivating within
them a strong sense of design and
aesthetics. As adults, their passion for
expression continues and their work is
enjoyed by art collectors nationwide.